Inexplicable Boundaries of *Love*

A journey down the path of the heart, transcribed in poetry.

W. T. RICHARDSON

ISBN: 978-1-4907-6114-5 (sc)
ISBN: 978-1-4907-6115-2 (hc)
ISBN: 978-1-4907-6116-9 (e)

Library of Congress Control Number: 2015909350

Trafford rev. 11/13/2015

 www.trafford.com
North America & international
toll-free: 1 888 232 4444 (USA & Canada)
fax: 812 355 4082

Contents

Dedication:

This book is a collection of works specifically written
for and dedicated to my smiley eyed muse,

My love and feelings for you will be eternal just as our friendship,
whether the stars align for us or not I will always be there for you.
Smiley eyes, I wish you true happiness, now and forever my love.
Thank you for teaching me to feel again.

- *Tommy*

Preface

Over my lifetime I have loved and lost many times over. With each heartfelt yearning and pain comes the desire to put my thoughts down in text. I do this as a way to express what I am feeling and provide an emotional release simultaneously giving me solace and sharing my inner self with that special someone. This book is a collection of poems written to a specific individual, just for her. I also searched through my previous ramblings and included some that I have on file that I choose to change and dedicate to her, as they read what I am feeling.

What you are about to read is not a literary masterpiece but a view, that until now, I was unwilling to share with the public. This provides the reader insight as to my thoughts, my soul, my inner being with which I am forever emotionally attached. Only through this text, am I able to convey the passion I hold so dear for her. Don't judge the writer or the muse, just deeply read the text and feel what is being said, not read.

Please open your heart and mind to achieve the emotion involved and reminisce in your past accounts of longing and desire. May you remember and relive each exquisitely enjoyable detail.

Thank you,
W.T. Richardson

Trials and Tribulations of Desire

Trial and tribulations day to day are abound,
constricting upon us round and round
Fun, laughter, joy, is there – funneling down as if from thin air
Commonality, truth, pure reality it is – bubbling up like soda fizz
One day, one step, from nature it comes –
not even known about by some
Actuality, existence, fact – it lays on each moment a bit of tact
How does it happen, and we keep asking when?
Playful, peaceful, solemnly it grows, go figure, still no one knows
The brightness is there, as the sun shines through her hair
Doubt, fear, joyful thoughts, and dreams –
fruition will it ever be as it seems?
Contemplate and believe, strive to see what has become,
something may be had but only for some
Those that feel, and know what is right, one
day – for that they resolve to fight
In depth they go and eventually realize – it is and
can be what they found in their eyes
Truth, soulful existence and realization must take
place – if ever reality they shall face
Inexplicable has it been found to be – the wonderful gift of her to me
Entering a life so stagnant and bleak – when a
shield melted and he first heard her speak
Inside the mind of a genius – even a lost
thought or feeling is meaningless
So speak and communicate their thoughts they have
done – While their eyes shown bright as the sun
Gleaming each minute and hour whilst time goes by –
endless it is and open -there future is a sky
Of wonder and peace, contentment and solace,
maybe one day they shall say a promise
Forever connected and protected are they, hearts and
minds together - a friendship that's surely here to stay.

What If?

I sit here and ponder the wonder of life
All the while continuing through the strife
A bond - Joy, smiles, laughter, love
Glistening as a rain drop on the wing of a dove
Minute after minute, hour after hour
As I pray that these sweet things will not sour
Thoughts, feelings, emotions swirling
Is it me? Or is the world spinning
Time is long and life is short
We always complain once the ship leaves port
To sail away in the distant sea
We incessantly ask "What could we be?"
Together as one we would figure it out
On standby, holding the water spout
Extinguish the fires that may come
Who cares what they say, or who it's from
Our lives we owe unto ourselves, happiness
Always avoid and steer away from the darkness

Think

Your ever so slight of touch draws me near
To your breathing and heartbeat I am close to hear
Your aura, your being, your presence controls me
I don't truly know, how that you can't see
I know you are full, and conflicted right now
Our needs, desires, wants; oh wow!
Your smile, your face, your hair, the epitome of perfection
Your eyes are glowing, for me a direction
My attention to you, your mind, your soul
My head, my mind, my heart starts to roll
Consistently when I am with you, as you've been told
I want to pull you to me, to embrace you and continue to hold
Onto what I believe is here, and what truly can be there
When oh when, and of course the where
Will we ever be free to be ourselves, not trapped
and fenced in by this binding force?
Please allow life, and other things to run their course
One day far from now, I don't wish to ever think
back to this time that we have now
Just to ask ourselves - we should have and didn't - What do we do now?
Regrets come and decisions go
A chance with you, I'd never blow
Think deep and think hard, for you and me
About just how happy, we really could be

Peace of Time

Starry nights above us continue to shine light
down upon your exquisite face
So delicate and soft I am unable to distinguish
it from a piece of fine silk lace
Lying on our sides and facing each other, dreaming of a life so grand
I love running my fingers through your hair
and feeling each single strand
Existing as and exemplifying pure beauty you are and always shall be
It means more than I can ever express, to have you close to me
Smiling, laughing, enjoying each breath we take together as we share
Each moment in time that exists which we have found is never truly fair
Destiny and fate have laid out the curves before each day begins
I start wondering what if, what is, ceases to be, shall
life start anew and all life's joys be taken in?
One day after the other is how we must tread,
sometimes I feel trodden and heavy as lead
One touch and one smile is always there to
lift me up and see the world of life
I almost want to begin marching to the drums and start playing a fife
At the top of my lungs I wish to scream, that you
are the one for I have always dreamed
Complicated is life and even more it becomes, as
I continue to type I become all thumbs ☺
My state is here and I want it to be there, I'm not sure if anymore I care
Numb is as my body and soul have turned, as though
my entire being were completely burned
Refresh and renew my soul you have done,
accomplished ever before by none
The greatest thanks to you I now truly owe, for
love and life is what you really do show
Those solid amber eyes always glowing so alive
each day, One day I'll be able to say......
What will become we shall see on the morrow,
for time is not a thing we can borrow

Never-ending Portals

Wandering and drifting day in and day out
Never ever needing to cry or pout
Bliss surrounds them
As the stalk, the stem
Supporting so strong and upright
Giving the beautiful gift of sight
Portals to the soul
Attention they hold
Deep and endless as the big blue sky
Are your gorgeous and perfect, beautiful eyes

Portals

Alive with feeling, constantly glowing
Open crevasse, door with no latch,
Full of emotion, as waves of the ocean
True inferno, few know though
Stairway inside, wonderful ride
Rooted in peace, soft as a fleece
Journey to eternity; certainly -
Flowing, controlling...
Asking, easing, wanting, waiting
To enter is bliss, a portal of light in the darkness

Our Trek

Your hair moves in the breeze & you seem such at ease
While you perch on a bench, awaiting your needs to be quenched
From the thirst for love & affection, your mind makes the connection
That peace is needed but loyalties should be heeded
Your eyes play a vision, creating a division
Of what's real you feel and with what you really deal
Each day in and day out, while you find out
That in your life you have someone, whom you've met equals none
That'll always be there, to play with your hair
And listen to the thought of how you've fought
To become who you are & how you've come so far
Through the trial of fire, of which each new day will sire
In life forever you will see, my heart will always continue to be
There when you have the need, it shall never require a plead
To have a chest upon which you may lay your head,
Where all your worries may be shed
Of all the superfluities of life, and I shall help you with your strife
Allow me the key to your best kept lock,
only then can we start the clock
Of the first day on our trek, to sort and explore the great train wreck
Of which all we see right now, just hang on while we find out how

Thank you

Thoughts and feelings swirling together in a mist,
thicker and richer it becomes each day
Some many things I want to share with you, to
please you and make you happy in every way
Each evolution continues to foster what I feel
for you, as endless as the sky is blue
Your beauty and mind all rolled into one, it is truly equal to none
Spinning, whirling, moving out of control, my heart
starts racing as I see the growing hole
You fill it each day that we are together, soft
and inviting as a baby down feather
I long for your touch and a sweet gorgeous smile,
that's what I've been awaiting, all this while
Your presence provides me the solace true love always
will, as beautiful as a rose at rest on a sill
The key is there, please let me inside, forever
you know – there's nothing to hide
Acceptance for who you are, without judgment,
I hope my love is the only solvent
To melt away the years of fear, open your heart
to me – each and every moment
Please continue to share with me what is inside of
you, for Love always finds a way to renew

Progression

Empty, barren, desolate – bleak
Words, feelings, thoughts – I can't speak
Joy, peace, pain, song
Smile, scream, cry – ring the gong
Time, direction, past, future
Help, support, love, nurture
Touch, squeeze, embrace, consummate
Fear, hate, stress, retaliate
Conjure, believe, realize, feel
Deny, ignore, accept what is real

Full

A perfect sphere amongst eternity
The glowing heart in the midst of fact
Facilitating the removal of all that is fiction
Shedding light unto the darkness
The same regardless of view
Thoughts, feelings, dreams co-mingling
Studied by me and absorbed by you
Natures cure to provide guidance
Solemn, pure, truth
Tonight it is as you make me
Rounded, whole, complete
We are one

Longing

Emotional satisfaction is upon us
Each and every thing for which we trust
In the hands of each other is golden
Whilst in the hands of any other is molten
In our lives we search a way
For when we can truly say
We will be together forever
Knowing our ties shall never sever
Enlightened I've become through you
For us, everything I now do
Wanting, longing, desire for your contact
Please let it be true that your feelings are fact
Our best will endeavor to endure
My love for you I am sure

Fear

Being around you I succumb to your brilliance
My longing to pull you close is in defiance
To touch you and caress your face
Only for the right time and place
Time passes and my heart grows fonder
All of these things I continue to ponder
My feelings for you are genuine
Glittering as a well placed sequin
Fluttery, warm and full of feeling
My pain is starting to send me reeling
From disaster I strive to keep myself
I cannot place it in a box on a shelf
To God I pray for a resolution
I'm seeing that only you can provide the solution
To my heart I am heavily leaning
My head still feels like it's pinging
My yearning for your companionship is ever growing
Even though the world passes by without ever knowing
My love for you is deeply rooted
I am scared that by you I will be booted
Out of your life and far away
Remnants of what could have been lay where they may
Show me sign that you are still there
Just tell me the truth, that you truly care
What happens between us in our future so bright
That will be my life in one night

Dreams

Such *a* beautiful and inviting face
I so long for your embrace
To have what really matters to each
Love is real, that I can teach
So far we are from where we've come
Our feelings for each other can be equaled by none
The timeline continues to run
My God, we'll have so much fun
Truth is the heart of our bond
Of you my heart is forever fond
Happiness lay on our road right now
Just say it, tell me how

Daydreams

It's all about you
That, I can only say for few
The daydreams are incessant
The feeling you provide is so pleasant
Warming and filling; at peace I feel
All day with you would be so real
To share with you the life that could be
If only it was just you and me

Answers

Your smile, your voice, your laughter
My mind, mind soul, my life you capture
In a net so tight I am more than willing
To allow you to keep on filling
My heart and head with your existence so great
I will no longer have an empty plate
Gather my thoughts I am trying
It feels so good to stop the lying
To myself that I have said over and over
My heart has been just a rover
Looking and searching for you until now
I have finally figured out the how

Future

Time passes
We need glasses
To see and realize you and me
One plus one equals We, maybe even three
Together operating
Forever contemplating
What next we do
To become me and you

Focus

Forced to peel open my eyes each day
One after another I must find a way
Feelings and thoughts are always hijacking
A straight line I am now really lacking
I must find a way to stay focused
Everything is approaching like a swarm of locusts
Convoluted is my way ahead
Please tell me how you feel instead
Of hiding it and shoving it away
I wait for the day I will hear you say
That all you want is to be with me
Together for all to see
Show me and tell me what is in your heart
That is only how we can start
To build the road to our future
Let's do it and stitch it as a suture
Seal it up and prep for healing
So never again will our hearts start reeling
From pain we've had in our past
For our love will forever last

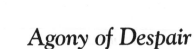

Agony of Despair

I want to scream, to run away, and to talk, I
want to cry, I want to hide in a hole,
I feel as though someone has numbed my soul,
The pain, the agony, yet no epiphany, will give me peace or solace
As much as being able to wake up to feel and see her face
Next to me and in my life, seems as though that will forever be my strife
Happiness may come and out it goes, ever to
return, for eternity - no one knows.

One Day

A breeze takes hold as precious as gold and forever, in my heart it holds
Such beauty, such grace, fine as lace, creating a trance I want to chant
I see, I feel, I desire, the wild fire tickles at my soul
The thoughts, the visions, the feelings invoked,
never clouded by the smoke
Of the burning, yearning, desire I have, to give you the world
Hoping, wishing, praying, that one day you will enter saying –
I know, I feel, I desire you too, let's break out of this zoo
To start a day together, hand in hand
Walking along a beach, our feet feeling the sand
Footsteps behind and bare ahead, lean upon
my breast your beautiful head
Know forever that on me you can rely, please don't ever be a bit shy
To call me by name and ask for assistance
You have already paid your penance
For whatever has come to pass, tell them to just kiss your ass
Forward and up we shall go, always happy for us to show
Where we came from and whom we are, the
fruit never really falls very far
From the source of it all, never stall - break down that wall
Keep moving and smile, laughing all the while
Let's have a life together, live and love in our very own style

Chemistry

Even though you push away, I can't help but to say
How much you truly mean to me,
If that, you really see
Or do you just have a switch inside
Always allowing you to run and hide
From the truth within your heart each day
Maybe it's just our minds at play
I know what I felt and how you responded in kind
Chemistry like that you don't just find
Out in a world so full of falsehoods
Think real hard you must and should
Be true to yourself, never fib
Even those thoughts so well you hid
Of what would happen if you took a chance
Maybe your life would start to dance
With joy and laughter each day abound
Finally making your being feel round
Complete is what you make me feel
Forever it shall take me to heal
Should you shut me out of your heart today
My love will completely stay
Focused on you and you alone
Through till my last dying bone

Another Time

Hours minutes days years
Following one after the other, creeping fears
Days in days out
No time to sit and pout
Will it be or will it not
Waiting for a boiling pot
With the heat and steam it grows
When it will stop hurting no one knows
For each second of each minute, it continues to fester
Only my mind does it ever pester
To find what is real and continue to feel
My life back for a moment I want to steal

Reality

To feel is to know, to know is to be
In your heart is where you must see
Troubles and concerns will melt away
We are real in every way
With each other, our beings are open
Trust is the forever token
To be placed in friend or lover
Never will we attempt to cover
Up anything we feel or do
That's the essence of being with you
Pure reality during each moment
We shall never be each other's opponent
Beauty lies in what we share
Truth is eternal for what we dare
To believe and know we are there forever
Lie to each other - that will be never

Shining

Shining ever so bright high in the sky
I continue to think and I really know why
Your smile, your laugh, your mind
Never before was it I could find
Someone who helps me get through each day
Your heart beating close to me helps me stay
Focused and atop the world abound
My forever friend and wanted lover I have now found
To touch you and embrace your being
Makes me feel as though I am king
Overjoyed and feeling just right
Ever wondering how to complete my plight
For true happiness and peace which you provide me
Over the course of time we shall see

Change

Doors open and the hallways are clear
Turning the corner and always in fear
Find the lights and hope they work
Yes, it's just another quirk
On and on they go like a maze
Ever growing like a starlight gaze
Which one will provide the need?
Which direction shall I have to heed?
Make a choice and do it fast
This door may be the last
To show itself while the lights are on
What will I do when it's all gone?

Reminder

A blissful summer day
Perfect in every way
A few clouds whisking around
Smiles and laughter are abound
Green grass and fresh air
A breeze slowly tickling your hair
Relaxation and peace overwhelming
Your presence is very calming
To my existence and my being
Is this what I am seeing?
Reality has a place
I'm reminded when I see your face
That my life is but a shell
Without you, it feels like hell

Depth

Black, brown, red, blonde, No matter, it is of your eyes I am fond
Sparkling, seeing, feeling, piercing; glowing with
knowledge, love, anguish, and truth
Only revealing to those that can see, like what
we can, when you look into me
The walls come down and no guards are there, truly it is only fair
To whit; I speak of "IT"
The truth, the essence, the soul, your eyes and their depth

Start

Days come and time flies by
Feelings, thoughts, and peaceful sighs
Rainbows, colors, drowning out the grey
Let it last and grow I pray
Sweet, blissful, calm understanding
Forever floating and never landing
Gliding amongst the stars so bright
The end is forever out of sight
Growing, nurturing, blending together
So light and airy, as that of a feather
Soft, subtle, exquisite
Life is the only pre-requisite
Two people, on one path with upheld heads
Life rolls out the road ahead
Hand in hand, heart in heart
When shall it really start?

A Rose?

Words, thoughts, feelings, tokens
Sometimes never require that they be spoken
Endlessly existing, constantly insisting
That an underlying presence is always persisting
A gift, a bud, of such wondrous color
Only given from and to a lover
Nurture it, and growth will avail
Its life a reminder, sharp as a nail
Tend it, over time you will see
Never shall it hurt you or me
Blossoming, the scents fill the air
Just as a breeze catches your hair
Warmth, emotion, beauty abound
Life is love, with which we surround
Each moment a stolen glance
I hope we truly have a chance
For real happiness and peace each day
Tell me please, what do you say?

Time

Click, tick, tock of the clock
Seconds, minutes, hours, go by
We incessantly wonder how and why
Why now and why not before?
Could we have known what life had in store?
For our wandering hearts and emotions have played
A wondrous game from day to day
Inside our thoughts, from behind a curtain
Now we realize how uncertain
Each step, each reach, can we - each other teach?
The way inside, deep down below
To one another whom we really know
To be so special and meaningful, our reality
Until now, our perception was seen through another's eyes,
Finally, away have gone all the lies
Before us now is a big cliff,
Can we, are we, should we, say What IF?
We take a chance and find it to be
The best thing ever for you and me

Dance of the Rose

Velvet, silk, sheer pleasure
Given, guarded, coveted treasure
Rare, exquisite, pleasantly adored
Volume, beauty, never ignored
Sharp, soft, a total package
Uplifting, brilliant, cures wreckage
Glowing, elegant, pure perfection
Enlightening, warming, gilded reflection
Now, then, eternal existence
Purposeful, deliberate, erotic stance
Alone, strong, absolute proof
100%, accurate, pure truth

Patience

Senses, touch, smell, feeling
Your presence sends me reeling
The slight jolt my heart receives
Every time my eyes, of you they see
The pleasing scent of you in the air
Adds the ever so special flare
Every moment of each day slows to a crawl
As I wait a time with patience to have you all
To myself and full attention I look forward to
When you and I finally say I do
To a world of uncertainty
Yet hope and dreams remain aplenty
Holding and grasping, each second we have with each other
Knowing that no one and nothing can ever smother
What we have is beyond special and sweet
Boldly put, it can't be beat

Favorite

Small and round yet still free flowing
Constantly flexing and always growing
Soft and subtle as a fresh snow while it falls
Majestic and bright, the power to tower over all
Grace, beauty, stealth abound
Never shall you know if I am around
Unless a time comes to pass when I am standing among the grass
For my true nature make me lie low
Amongst the beautiful tufts of snow
A heartbeat lies between you and me
For it will disappear if you don't find me
Because I will find you and be the winner
For you will become my latest dinner

My Friend

Good-bad-indifferent, right-wrong- either way
My mind wanders, each and every day
Some of dreams, some of reality
Far away, from this principality
To a time of peace, a life of solace
The same way I feel, when I see your face
A feeling, an unspoken word, a realization
The breadth and width of which, could swallow a nation
Warmth, gratitude, appreciation for now
It's here, It is, yet we still wonder how
Life is upon each thought
To get here, we have always fought
To be, to become, what others can see
There is and always will be, more than that of you and me
A bond, a tie, a will so strong
To stand up and stray from wrong
Smiles and laughter fill our minds
You truly are, One of a kind

Normal?

I think, I wonder, I truly ponder
Today, tomorrow, all of eternity
The highs, the lows, somewhere between
Where in life can it be seen?
Do this, do that, let's have a chat
Go here, go there, they often begin to stare
Him, her, whomever it is
Ragged, worn, nicely formal
What on earth is really normal?

Chance

Incessantly contemplating, forever generating
Ideas, imaginations, and correlations
Fervor, excitement, and restraint
A sound, a choice, the one true voice
Reflection, selection, perfection
Waiting, wanting, yearning
To touch, just such – as to join
The inner being of one another
In an embrace, face to face
Ever seeing and really believing
Today is here and would always come
Only dreamed about by some
The day when it takes hold
When life begins to be so bold
Thrown into the fire we are
Out we will come, without a scar
Wounds heal and pain goes away
Always I am, with you to stay

Life

Do we yes, or do we know?
Neither has the ability to show
Which is right and which is wrong?
Can we find it in a song?
A song so sweet, pure, and real
I feel as though I'm under a keel
Being dragged through life, it can't be real
Why would we be allowed to find
One of each, each, one of a kind
To love and have to forever hold
Yet, for each at times it must feel so cold
To have to back away and turn the fold
Each page is there before us, some empty and some not
We have a chance to write our own plot
Our hearts continue to resist, sometimes we must just exist
One day at a time we said
To always be there, I hereby pledge
For you, I will stay true
True to life and true to my heart,
Each day is a brand new start
What to do and what to say
Obviously I can't have it my way
But to have you here and know your heart divides
That is where my pain resides
Agony, anguish, ultimate despair
Life truly is, not very fair
To allow us to feel and then totally ignore, what our soul has to say
Time will tell and takes its toll
Such as the order of things, continues to roll
I pray that we never part,
For you will always have my heart

Inside

I sit and watch you smile that gorgeous grin
The day passes and the night comes 'round
I can't help but think and dread the when
Of the time you walk away and there is no more a sound
Of your sweet and elegant voice in the air
I wish and want to have you near
That I start to feel empty and drawn with despair
Hopefully one day however it goes, your life will be clear
To enable you to be free from the confusion
Of whatever is in your head flashing by
I just want what you feel, and whatever you do, to not be an illusion
That leaves you sitting, waiting, in 30 years asking WHY?
I want you happy, pure truth to survive
To be true to yourself and only you
Your heart is precious and it may be revived
By who, or when, if only you just knew
What to do and what to say, from your head to your heart
The action of speaking what is inside your mind now
Some words are hard and may even be tart,
You lay there and continue to just wonder how
What to do, I pray, may your head become quiet
I wish you peace and solace inside
Find your way and just stand by it
I know you are strong, like the big ocean tide
Moving everything and never yielding
To anything other than that of love
Forever you heart, strongly shielding
The soft and beautiful nature of your soul

Expression

Soft, exquisite, a breathtaking view is laid upon the altar each day
The hues, the warmth, the brightness that approaches in every way
Time stands still, frozen, acquiring permission to move forward
What's that? OH yes! I am graced, for your voice I have now heard
Sweet as honey drops, with dark chocolate on a cake
Enlightened, special, you are one for which my life I'd forsake
Give up and give in, to whatever happens, I will
If only I could say, you'd be with me still
Lovers, friends, partners, whichever we may in the future become
We would have what no other has, not even some
The bond, the tie, and truth that sets us free
For a life that could be so enthralling, with just you and me
Today, tomorrow, next year, or whenever
My heart, my mind, my life shall not waiver
From being open, honest, and true with you
Even our favorite color is blue! ☺
Laughing, smiling, living life as we may
No regrets and no qualms, that we can say
Is what carries us on from day to day
Heads up high and hearts running strong
When I am with you, nothing ever feels wrong
Someday, I'd like to celebrate with a song
On my sax I will play, just for you that day
With music, sound, and my heart I shall say
Something that I repeatedly must tell you
From my heart and mind, I truly love you.

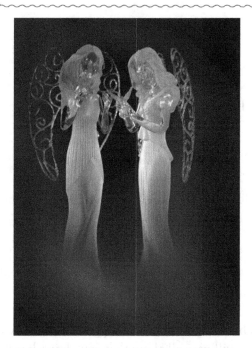

Sculpture of an Angel

The finest of lead crystal is set upon the stage
The tools are laid out, one by one according to age
An imagination so clear, of the most perfect piece
Each curve is chiseled, piece by piece
Time and great care go into each stroke as the rhythm increases
The work goes on and on, it just never ceases
Each petal begins to take its shape
All behind the fine silk drape
One by one, two by two, the stems and leaves come alive
All at once they begin to thrive
On life, smiles, and love they are there
Each and *every* nuance is now laid bare
Sun setting, moon rising, a drop of dew exists
Forever they will continue to persist
As the example of beauty you have always shown
You are the most gorgeous flower I have ever known

Transitions

I am your friend now, and always will be,
Although I long to have you near me
To look deep into my eyes and say
You want me by your side in every way
I know what you want right now,
That may last forever, I do understand how
Don't ever think that just because
I may shut my mouth, that it was
Due to me not truly knowing how I feel
The love I have for you is the realest of real
If ever you do change your mind,
I truly wish you to find
That I will have never stopped caring for you
I will pray all along that you always knew
All I pray for and really want for you
Is the happiness that you deserve so true
I am and always will be,
The other half of the friendship, of you and me

My Mind

My mind is blank, yet racing, my heart is numb, yet pacing,
I don't know what has happened, just that
the sky seems to have blackened
To do, to say, stay away from the fray, Oh help me get through this day
To try and be the one that I should be, passed
this moment I'm trying hard to see
signs, signals, of life's long road ahead, I feel
as though all night I have bled
Out of desperation and agony I have emerged,
my feelings seem so deeply submerged
The want, the desire, My heart is on fire, To
be so free and out of the mire
Of the times and trials that are so evident,
why is the next step so dependent
On whatever happens now, the garden of life needs a plow
To turn the soil that's hard as a stone, what
will it feel like to be all alone
Days pass by and I idly meander, please may I get out from under
The rock that lies upon my soul, day after day taking its toll
My heart is dividing and providing a view, of
what I really want, and that is you.
In my current state I feel numb to all things, until
I think of you and your beautiful wings.
The angel that has come into my life, standing
beside me through my strife
My love, my friend, my beacon, you are my angelic
flower, you have no idea of the power
That you bestow upon me, I truly hope that you can see
Exactly how important it is, that I know my
friend is beside me, all through this
Thinking of you begets me peace, and then all the pain starts to cease
At least for a few moments of my day, I get to daydream of it that way
Of a time that has yet to come, it may never happen or remotely come
Close to emerging as a reality but that's
okay, For I truly love you anyway.

Rings on the Water

Each drop starts a ring to expand
Lovingly holding each hand in hand
To stand together so free and bare
As if it just came out of thin air
Tightly gripping onto what they know
Will ever a day come that they can show
Each and every way in their hearts
Only one chance it takes to start
Finding and realizing a most unclear path
One must only do the math
From here to there and everywhere
Each moment is so special that they do share
Friends and minds combine together
That each wishes it will last forever
A long time, that statement holds so true
One day at a time, for me and you
As we ponder and wander the road ahead
We think and dream each night in bed
How may we strive to make this stay
We need each other in every way
To listen and be a shoulder to lean on
Even if we need one just to cry on
For a bond that we have there is no likeness
Let's go forward into the wilderness
The woods filled will blossoms so bright
How strong we are, it's out of sight
From anyone that just doesn't understand
We are there to hold each other's hand
In times of despair and times of glory
I think you see the moral of this story
Friends we are, so close, how great
You have put me into a glorious state
Of mind from each day I know you
Your heart is just so true

I find that I love that the best
As time is the only real test
Of a friendship such that we have developed
My heart and soul it has enveloped
To be true and honest in all that I do
So long as it all pertains to you
Your eyes, those entrancing pearls of beauty and wisdom
Have given me the utmost free of freedoms
To speak my mind and know you will hear
Losing you is my only fear
Such a great thing it is that we are
In life, it shows just how far
We have now come and need to go
How I feel, this, you already know
Love aside and even a ring,
I wouldn't trade this for anything
You mean more than I can express at all here
Thank you for being there, from year to year
For a time has passed since this all began
Do it all over, I would again and again
To have you here and close to me,
Just so that I could truly know thee
In the heart, we are extremely connected in life
I will listen to many, and every, and all of your strife
That you may know and love the freedom of release
Just never forget I am here for you, please
In any and all fashions galore
Just tell me if you ever need more
Than an endearing look, or hand to help you stand
I promise I will ever hold your hand

Unknown

Over rated, slightly abated
Swimming high and drifting low, when it stops, no one knows
Ramblings, thinking, incessant weeping
Minutes, hours, days, let me count the ways
In which you make me feel
Utterly, unfathomably, really real
Full of emotion and swelling inside
When oh when shall we take a ride
On the road to happiness from which we shall see
Whatever will become of you and me

View

Rose petals unfolding, reaching high
The sun rising over a mountain top
Blossoms and berries abound with perfect fecundity
Coming to life for all to see
Spring's gentle flower, a scent of beauty
Strong in the wind, delicately swinging in the breeze
Beautiful, gorgeous all the while
None come close to your elegant smile

Lost

What an epiphany
Downtrodden and bleak
Happiness is all I seek
A hole has opened up
Once more an empty cup
Lies in my life
It's forever my strife
To know and lose what is so precious
Only to be one of the wretches
That knows what it means to lose from above
A thing as special as the one called love

Feelings

Quiet, silence, nothing
Thoughts, ideas of self-worth
What if, what now, wow
Wondering, hovering, fears
Emotions, commotion, tears
Moods, personas, personalities
Life's unkind realities

A Letter from My heart

I know why I feel this way
I don't know what I should really say
Except all the thoughts that pop into my head
Most of which I've already said
Some remain, buried within
If they'll come out, I won't know when
Unknown they are, as of yet
You'll be the first to know, no need to bet
You have unlocked a door, long thought to have disappeared
For your voice, I long to hear
That you understand how I really feel
As long as you know what is there is real
My heart, my love, and my mind you have captivated
Never in my life has my heart been resuscitated
As it was by you, with the time we've had
No, never, could this ever be bad
This is a love and friendship, like no other in existence
I only hope it's realized, through this remittance
Of work on paper in poetic form
Yes, I know this is not the norm
Of society, relationships, bonds of view
I am happy that we have something new
To share and blossom in each of our lives
Our friendship, always to protect I will strive

"making love is". It's spiritual, yet passionate, at the same time. Our intellectual, genuine approach for one another from when we first [...] the purest form of affection that I have ever experienced. [...] However, [...] see, I am hopelessly lost. Like been a very strong person, [...] a little child that above [...] it's right [...] Occasion I can hear you in the house and for a moment [...] in the world, I haven't thanked you lately for [...] your [...] the ghost keeps me company for a few seconds [...] while your ghost, I wake up in the morning and hear your [...] or in the shower, or I don't smell your perfume but it's [...] but I thank God for that ghost. Every time I feel it [...] your one only soul make, you [...] shared, even more there before, I have [...] that neither of us truly knew what [...] see it, we passion was before we [...] overwhelming first done to that one [...] You are I ever come to it. You are [...] and my heart and soul — never [...] loving heart I am truly sorry [...] without letting you know how [...]

It has [...] been one and [...] you in my arms and it has [...] into each other's eyes and [...] sincere friendship turned into [...] out the true meaning of love [...] sometimes and [...] some [...] is purposely [...] and stretching [...] making us [...] and faith [...] distance relation [...] a lot. From this [...] what it is [...] completely to the [...] when you're too far [...] the most importants things [...] more things was [...] trust and to be faithful to the one [...] love chatting with you on the internet and [...] good night, but in my heart I doubt I want [...] frozen that minute before we have to [...] enjoy every single moment with you, [...] all of the thing we like and dislike [...] lollipop that I Round I like to [...] Boy, I want your brother bought for [...] me when I really will [...] and writing to tell you [...] that [...] come back you've [...] the way [...] work later and [...] know that this letter [...]

Frustration

My thoughts intermingle upon the sands of time
Emotions swirling with life they intertwine
Themselves into the abyss of the unknown
Over and over again I've been shown
Keep to myself my heart I really should
Because of what they really could
Do to it should ever I let them
Just stomp on it and crush it as a stem
Only I am to blame for this feat
I will accept it as they cover me with a sheet
When the day comes that I am no more
All will know at their very core
That I have lived a life of bliss,
Celebrated by the benevolent kiss
Of friendship and love that I felt so well
Until that day I must endure the hell
Of knowing that they don't want to be around
Or even really just hear a sound
From, away, or even about me they run
As though straying from the burning sun
It's okay I say to them as they reel
Pretty soon I won't even feel
The numb of life just takes it away
I love you is the last thing I say

Printed in the United States
By Bookmasters